ROCKET AROUND *Switzerland!*

A neurodiverse-friendly visual guide for kids

Written by
Lee Lynch

Illustrations by
Emma Lynch

Contributors
Jeffrey, Jack, & Tom Lynch

Guest Appearance
Dottie

ROCKET AROUND LLC   U.S.A.

This book is for neurodiverse and neurotypical kids around the world of any age, who love adventure, imagination, and finding new ways to have fun!

Neurodiverse people behave, think, and learn differently from people with neurotypical brains. These differences include strengths. In a word, neurodiverse people are awesome. Neurodiverse people might be autistic, live with ADHD, dyslexia, PTSD, Tourette's, or other things.

Safety Tips

Being safe when you travel is important. Remember to:

-Keep the adult you're with in sight
-Set a place to meet in case you cannot find your adult
-Know their phone number - write it here: _____
-If you feel lost, ask a police officer or information desk for help
-If your family has an emergency when in Switzerland, call phone number 112 (that's like 911 in the U.S.)

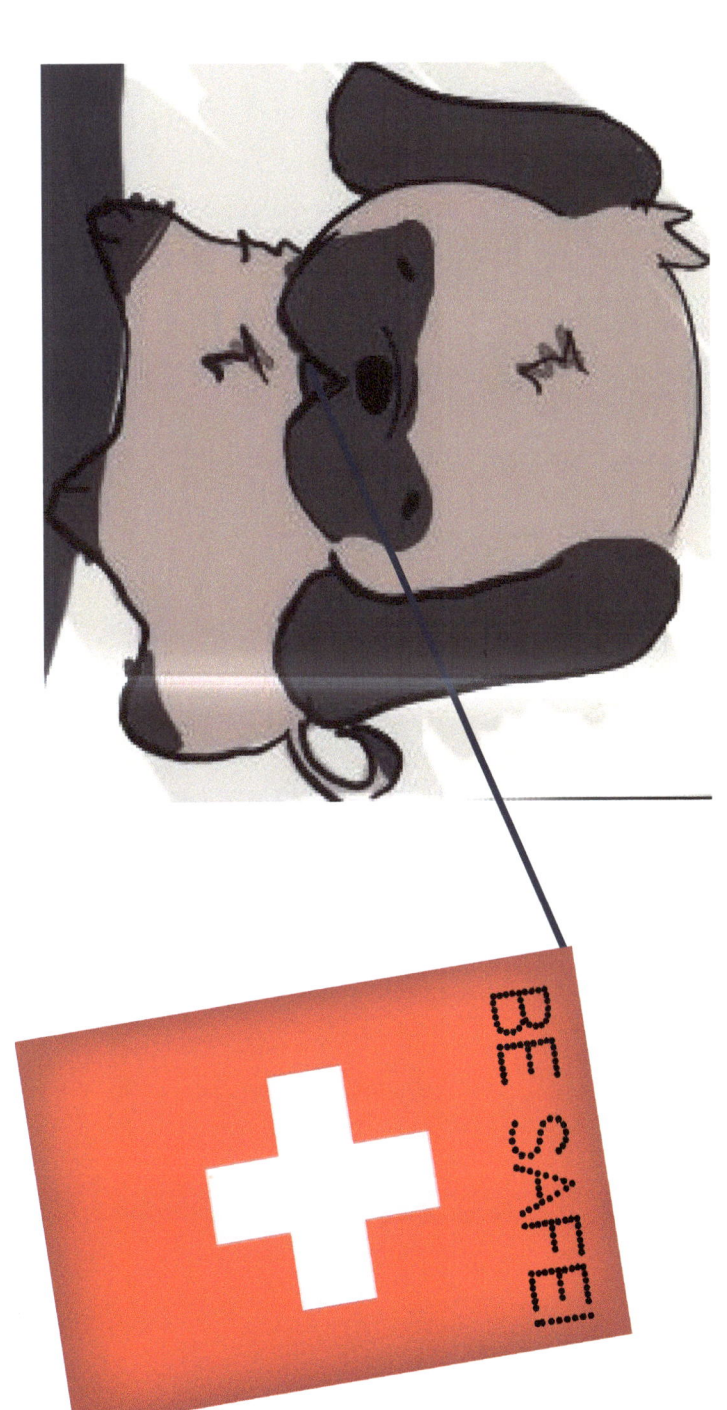

BE SAFE!

Everywhere We Go in This Book...

You can also see where all of the above sites are located on the map on Pg. 32

Everywhere We Go continued

See page 47 to be a ROCKETAROUNDER!

Guten tag travel friend!

Guten tag means good day in German.

Why am I talking to you in German?

My neurodiverse family is going to Switzerland, and in some parts of that country, they speak German.

You remember my human family – Jeffrey, Jack, Emma, Dad, and Mom.

They've planned this trip for a while, and it sounds awesome!

They think I'm staying with a dog sitter, but I'll just switch myself for this Rocket stuffie in Emma's backpack.

Here we go!

Phew. Made it through security and onto the airplane! I think I'll help the flight attendants – cookies anyone?

I LOVE flying! So many fun things to do – watch movies, play games, get petted by people around me, eat, and sleep.

Now the pilot is about to land the plane in Geneva, Switzerland. I'd better get in the backpack!

What do you like to do on an airplane?

(See page 39 for Rocket's favorites)

Here we are – Geneva, Switzerland. Bonjour! They speak French in this part of Switzerland because we are right across the lake – Lake Geneva – from France!

Geneva is an old city – it's been around since <u>1 BC</u> – that's more than two thousand years! There are so many things to do here. What's your favorite thing to do in Geneva?

Hey, isn't that the flight attendant from the airplane?

Here are 5 of my favorites things to see in Geneva:

1. Sit (sail, or bike) along Lake Geneva and watch the humans and other dogs walk by, while you look out at the snow-covered mountains. Watch the water jet fountain (Jet d'Eau in French) shoot water up to 450 feet (140 meters) in the air – WOW!

2. Walk around the city, from chocolate shop to chocolate shop – Swiss chocolate is the best!

3. Sniff the [Flower Clock in the English Garden park](#) (in French, it's called the L'horloge fleurie in the Jardin Anglais park).

4. Visit one of Geneva's cool museums, like the Exploracentre science center, Natural History Museum or International Museum of the Red Cross and Red Crescent.

5. Wander around the Medieval Old Town (in French, it's called the Vieille Ville) – a maze of narrow ancient streets.

Oh no – my family is getting on the train! Looks like they're heading to…

Fast Fact

Lausanne Is the home to the International Olympic Committee (IOC), a group of humans who organize every Olympic Games, and is a really interesting place to visit!

What's your favorite sport?

Ouchy Promenade

Lausanne, Switzerland – a beautiful city on the other side of Lake Geneva from Geneva.

Lausanne, like Geneva, is old. About 2000 years ago, it was part of the Roman Empire, but a scary group called the Barbarians invaded, and the people who lived there ran into the nearby hills.

Today, Lausanne has an <u>Old Town</u>, which is where people lived 2000 years ago, and a New Town, in the hills. They're connected by a metro train. My humans are rocketing around Lausanne – let's follow them!

There they are – strolling along the Ouchy promenade, between the Old Harbor – which looks across to France – and the Old Town. Look, they're on those swings – wait for us!

Olympic Museum

Now they're on the move again and going into the Olympic Museum.

It has stories, videos, costumes, medals, and other things from all the different Olympic Games, and it has many interactive activities for kids of all ages.

Look, Emma won a gold medal, and Dad took the silver. Go team! Looks like they're heading to the metro to go to the Old Town – allons-y! (that's let's go in French).

This metro is great – so much easier on the paws than walking up these hills.

They're getting off here and heading to the Cathedrale de Lausanne – the largest Gothic-style building in Switzerland

It sits on Cite hill, one of the three hills of the city. Now they're walking through these windy, stone streets and now down a really long staircase – market staircase (Escaliers du Marche in French).

In old days, it made a path between the old city's two markets. Today there are food shops and restaurants.

Cathedrale de Lausanne - The windows are pieces of art that show things like months of the year.

Cathedrale de Lausanne

Market staircase

Looks like my humans are going into a restaurant that smells like CHEESE! As you know, that's my favorite food. It's a fondue restaurant. Fondue means melted in French. I've always wanted to try fondue – don't mind if I do fondue!

Have you heard of Swiss cheese?

You can get it wherever you live.

What to Eat

Swiss fondue is the country's most famous dish.

Fondue is melted cheese that you dip bread and other foods into.

YUM!

Fondue

14

My humans are on the move again – let's go! Looks like they're walking to the Place de la Palud.

Look – the market is open. Let's get some delicious cake, sausages and of course MORE CHEESE!

They're over at Lausanne City Hall, built 400 years ago. And right there is the Fountain of Justice, and here's the wall clock, built for the 1964 Swiss Exposition.

Sniff sniff...smells like my humans area heading toward...

Place de Palud and Fountain of Justice

Grand-Pont, which used to be called the Pont Pichard bridge. The bridge used to be two stories and about 75 feet (25 meters) high, but years ago the bottom level was covered over in dirt. The arches remind me of a doorway. Wait, where are my humans? Sniff sniff – smells like they've headed over to the Church of Saint Francois.

This church was first built about 900 years ago, burned down after only 100 years, then was built again into what you see today.

What to See

Church of Saint Francois: See the gold stones in front of the church? Each stone represents a little human born in Lausanne on a full moon night in the year 1998. How many do you see?

(see page 37 for fun facts about Lausanne and other places we visit in Switzerland)

Grand-Pont

Hey, my humans have their luggage and are heading to the train station – looks like we're rocketing somewhere new!

I love riding the train – so comfy.

The country has more than 3,000 miles of railway, and all of it runs on electricity.

A lot of the electricity used for Swiss trains is water powered.

I'm just going to sneak under this seat and take a quick nap. Zzzzzzz.

And now we're pulling into…

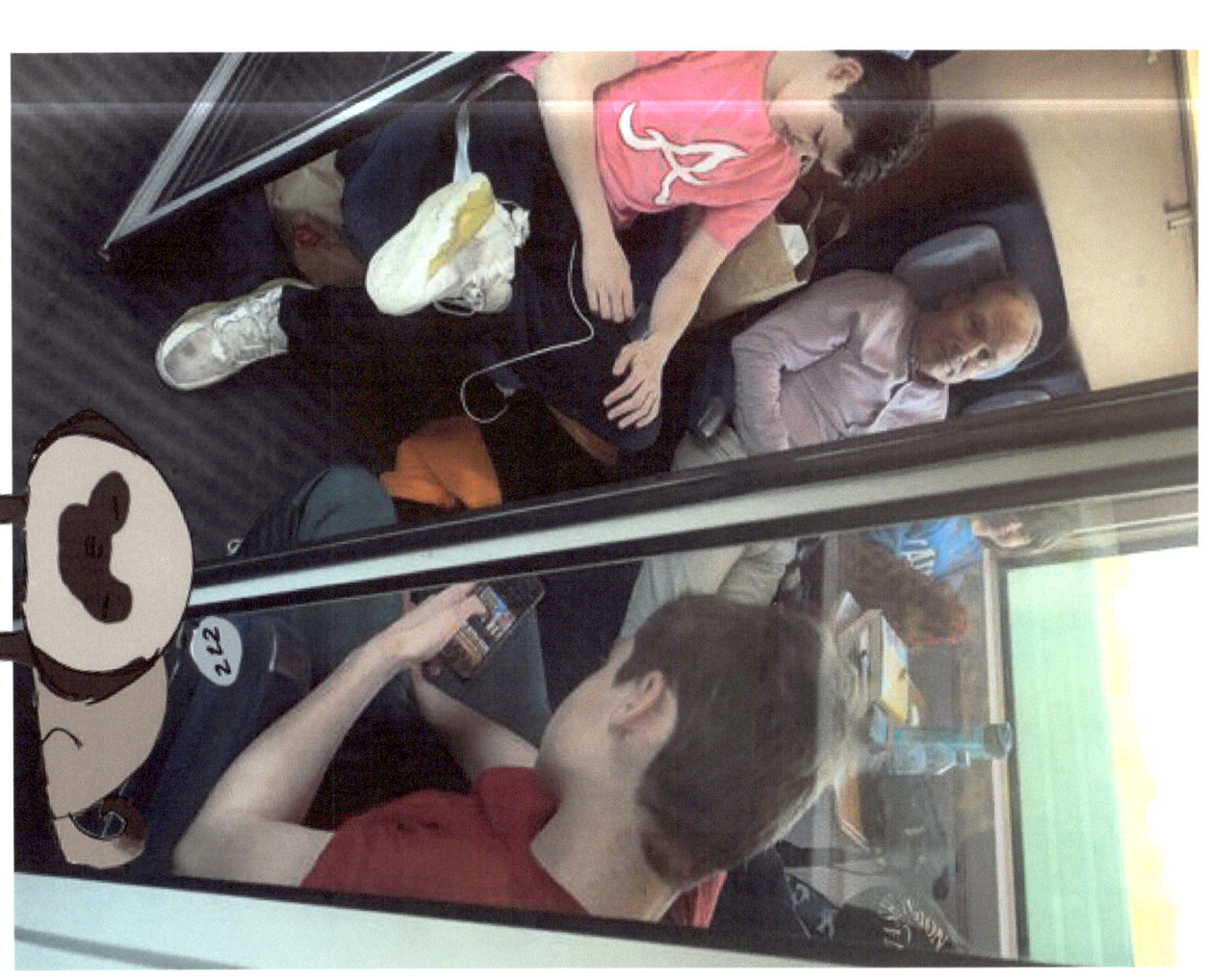

Old Town Lucerne

Lake Lucerne

Lucerne, where they speak German.

Guten tag! (that's good day in German)

I can't wait to get into Old Town Lucerne– it's the best!

There are my humans – strolling along the river Reuss, which flows into the harbor of Lake Lucerne.

Everywhere you look, you see something beautiful.

Bridges and colorful buildings that are hundreds of years old, the harbor leading out to Mount Burgenstock, and Mount Riga and Mount Pilatus which are parts of the amazing Swiss Alps.

Now they're heading over to Mill Square (Mühlenplatz in German) to see where the city's water wheels take flowing water and turn it into [energy for almost 1,000 houses](#). Mill Square has had water and water wheels for almost 900 years! My humans are moving on to some of Lucerne's bridges – let's go!

Old Town Lucerne has five bridges so that people can cross the river Reuss. My humans are walking across the Spreuer Bridge (Spreuerbrücke in German), which has more than 45 paintings in the ceiling.

*Mill
Square*

Spreuer Bridge

Chapel Bridge

They've moved onto Lucerne's most famous bridge – Chapel Bridge (Kappelbrücke in German). Hold on looks like they're heading out of Old Town to the Swiss Museum of Transport (or Verkehrshaus der Schweiz) – and why not?

What to See

Chapel Bridge - It's Europe's oldest wooden bridge, but a lot of it had to be rebuilt after a boat sitting underneath it caught fire. You can tell this bridge by the small chapel in the middle of it that is almost 500 years old.

It shows and tells how different kinds of Swiss transportation work, from trains, automobiles ships, and aircraft. It's the most popular museum in Switzerland!

Swiss Transport Museum

Look how much fun they're having – working on a construction site for a transportation project, driving the metro, touring through all of the cool cars and trains. Come on – there are hundreds of fun things here to do – let's do them all!

Swiss Transport Museum

Oh geez - have to move on – looks like my humans are heading to the Port of Lucerne and getting on the ferry to go to Mount Bürgenstock – jump!

Now it's just a quick trip across Lake Lucerne to Bürgenstock, a mountain we get to the top of by taking a funicular (a cable railroad, that goes up a mountainside) almost straight up. Or you could take the road but the funicular is more fun!

You can look across the lake to Lucerne and into the mountains.

Over there is another famous Lucerne site – the Musegg Wall and its nine Towers. Look how beautiful the view is!

Mount Bürgenstock Funicular

Lake Lucerne

You can look across the lake to Lucerne and into the mountains.

Hey look - it's another pup - a Bernese Mountain Dog. They come from the Swiss Alps. She'll know her way around here!

Hi, I'm Dottie!

Wait, they're LEAVING? Come on Dottie - my humans are heading back across Lake Lucerne and I hear them saying they are going to...

<u>Mount Pilatus</u> – let's go, we won't want to miss that! What a trip - my humans took a bus, then walked up a big hill to an air gondola (which looks like an amusement ride on a cable) and now are on a bigger air gondola.

Air gondola to Mount Pilatus

Mount Pilatus

Whoa, we just broke through the clouds! Mount Pilatus is right in front of us, and the Alps - the longest mountain range in all of Europe – and the countryside is all around us!

Time for some selfies! Smile Dottie!

Mount Pilatus

Pic of Rocket and Dottie!

The Alps stretches across seven countries.

Mount Pilatus

Somehow on the mountain, there are flags planted by hikers and there's even a church - they look like they're in impossible places for humans to get to.

I could get up there, but how would a human do it?

Look at Jack throwing snowballs down the Alps.

Glad we have our fur on – it's cold up here!

I think we should spend some time here, hiking around, and watching the birds soar across the sky.

Mount Pilatus and Swiss Alps

Is that Rocket with a Bernese Mountain Dog?

Oh no, my humans are heading down the mountain. Let's go Dottie!

They're heading to the train station! Dottie, thanks for rocketing around with us - we'll see you next time we're in the Swiss Alps.

Looks like the train is pulling into Zürich! I can't wait to tour this amazing city.

They speak German here, which is gut (good in German) because I've learned some German phrases on our trip (you can learn more German phrases on page 40).

Everywhere you look there's a pretty site.

There's Lake Zürich, the Old Town which sits on both sides of the Limmat river, the colorful houses, old churches, courtyards, narrow alleys, and clocks all over the place.

City of Zurich

Limmat river

Zurich has so many parks, playgrounds, museums, churches. There's even a church on an island on Lake Zürich.

And there are many places to get cheese and chocolate.

One of the big chocolate factories even has a 30-foot chocolate fountain!

I think I'll doggie paddle in it for a while.

City of Zurich

Fast Facts

Germany is located north of Switzerland.

It is nine times bigger than Switzerland and has about 10 times as many people.

Switzerland has four official languages - German, French, Italian, and Romansh. Germany has one - German.

No more time for that now – my humans are on the move. They're getting back on the train. I wonder where we're going next?

I love looking out at the beautiful Swiss countryside. Wait, did that sign just say Welcome to Germany?

Are we going to rocket around GERMANY? Auf Wiedersehen (good bye in German) for now!
To be continued...

SpaÃŸ! (FUN! in German)

Switzerland

Match the numbers to the sites on the next page.

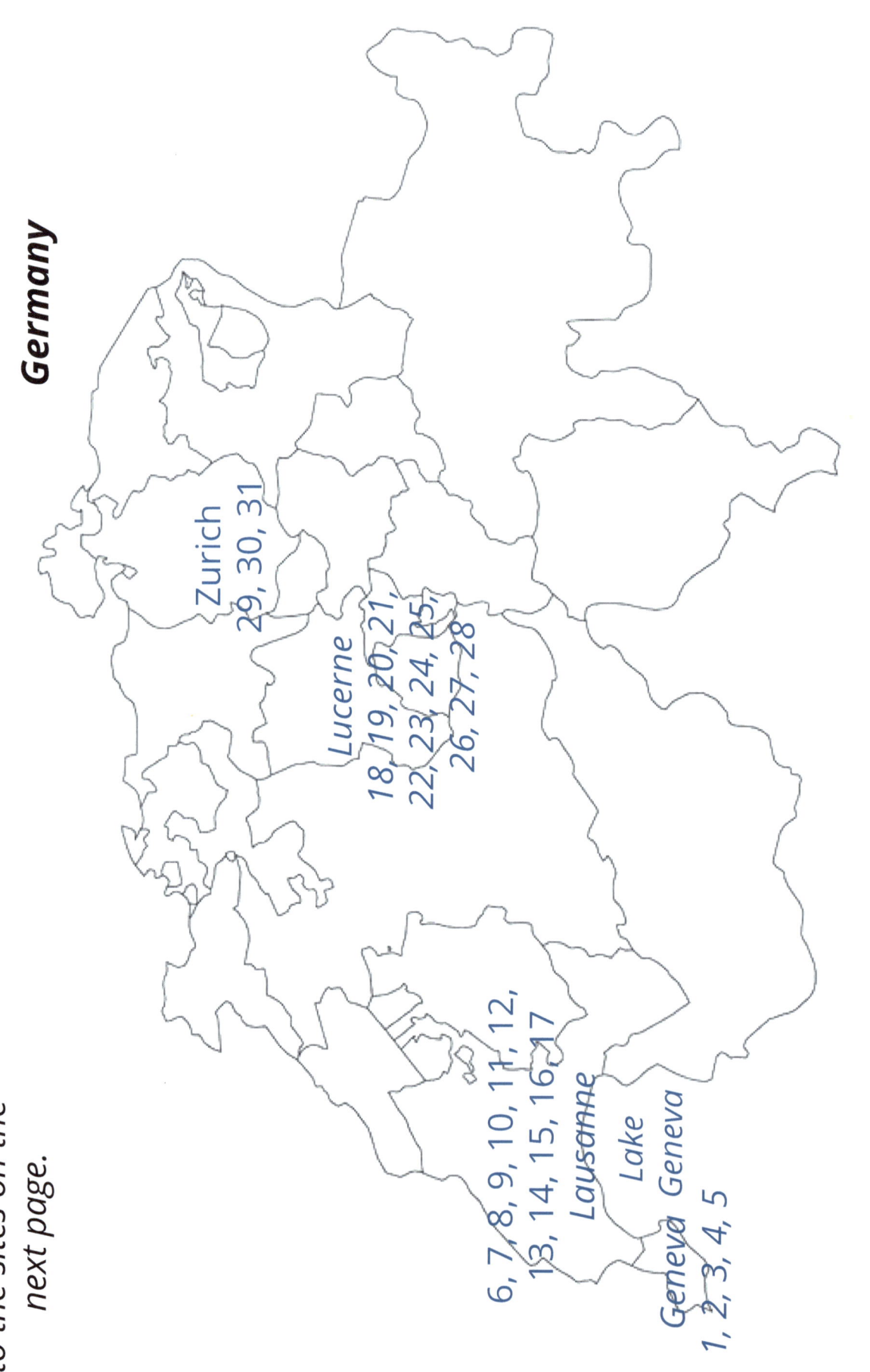

Germany

Zurich
29, 30, 31

Lucerne
18, 19, 20, 21,
22, 23, 24, 25,
26, 27, 28

6, 7, 8, 9, 10, 11, 12,
13, 14, 15, 16, 17

Lausanne

Lake
Geneva

Geneva
1, 2, 3, 4, 5

Geneva:
1. Water jet fountain
2. Flower Clock English Garden park
3. Exploracentre science center
4. Natural History Museum
5. International Museum of the Red Cross and Red Crescent

Lausanne:
6. Ouchy Promenade
7. Old Harbor
8. Olympic Museum
9. Cathedrale de Lausanne
10. Cite hill
11. Market staircase
12. Restaurant with fondue
13. Place de la Palud
14. Lausanne City Hall
15. Fountain of Justice
16. Grand-Pont
17. Church of Saint Francois

Lucerne:
18. Old Town Lucerne
19. River Reuss
20. Lake Lucerne
21. Mount Burgenstock
22. Mount Pilatus
23. Mill Square
24. Spreuer Bridge
25. Chapel Bridge
26. Swiss Museum of Transport
27. Port of Lucerne
28. Swiss Alps

Zurich:
29. Lake Zürich
30. Limmat river
31. Chocolate Fountain

Word Search

(Answers on next page)

Find these words in the puzzle

Alps	Lausanne
Bridge	Limmat
Burgenstock	Lucerne
Chapel	Mountain
Cheese	Pilatus
Chocolate	Plane
Geneva	Rocket
Harbor	Switzerland
Lake	Train
Lake	Zurich

Add extra words you find here:

_____

_____

_____

```
S Q Q C O J K L H H A S Z Q R O C K E T
S N W H I B D C J Y R U E W D U Z H A W
T L E O K O E D O C H E E S E Z O V R G
O B F C J F P E B F E R N S Z J R A Z J I
L N K O T M O X M Y X F S Z I Y H M E Y
N U W L H A R B O R T S M O U N T A I N
X J L A L P G T M W R E E F L E K B B
Y Z I T W H X U O D A X F A D A N Z C C
C D M E V F H O D O I R F B K K Q K X B
R H M P T B W L J U N R N T K E L Z J P
P W A O Z U R I C H U G E N E V A L R J
P B T L M O V G D B O L O R W G U B N G
L D P B S L Z R Q A B A O I L L S N E Q
A N Z I S R A T Q D R K V P I L A T U S
N F F R J O W A J E X M Y Y N C U X
E A S R N X F Q N U E C F F O X N V C U
E S C K F B R I D G E L O L U C E R N E
M T L F H P W I X V Z M R B V Y H K Q I
S W I T Z E R L A N D X U O A L P S P Z
B U R G E N S T O C K C H A P E L G U Y
```

34

ANSWERS FOR Word Search

Word list:

- Alps
- Bridge
- Burgenstock
- Chapel
- Cheese
- Chocolate
- Geneva
- Harbor
- Lake
- Lake
- Lausanne
- Limmat
- Lucerne
- Mountain
- Pilatus
- Plane
- Rocket
- Switzerland
- Train
- Zurich

Fun Facts about Switzerland

Draw a line from the fact on the left to the correct site on the right. (Answers on next page)

Facts

The water fountain (Jet d'Eau) in this city shoots water 125 miles per hour!

6,500 flowers and bushes are used to create the face of this in Geneva.

This yummy cheese dish is the national dish of Switzerland.

This staircase made a path between two markets of Lausanne's old city.

Located in Lausanne, this is the largest freshwater aquarium in Europe.

This Lausanne museum has about 1,500 objects from different Olympics.

These mountains stretch across 65 percent of Switzerland.

A long wooden horn that helped people living in the Alps communicate.

Switzerland has 3,000+ miles of this, all running on electricity.

Sites

The Alps

Zurich

Fondue

The Olympic Museum

Railway

Market staircase

Aquatis

Geneva

Alpine horn (or alphorn)

Flower Clock

ANSWERS for Fun Facts about Switzerland

Facts and Answers

The water fountain (Jet d'Eau) in this city shoots water 125 miles per hour! **Geneva**

6,500 flowers and bushes are used to create the face of this in Geneva. **Flower Clock**

This yummy cheese dish is the national dish of Switzerland. **Fondue**

This staircase made a path between two markets of Lausanne's old city. **Market staircase**

Located in Lausanne, this is the largest freshwater aquarium in Europe. **Aquatis**

This Lausanne museum has about 1,500 objects from different Olympics. **The Olympic Museum**

These mountains stretch across 65 percent of Switzerland. **The Alps**

A long wooden horn that helped people living in the Alps. **Alpine horn (or alphorn)**

Switzerland has 3,000+ miles of this, all running on electricity. **Railway**

This is Switzerland's largest city. **Zurich**

Rocket's Top 10

1. Eat
2. Sleep
3. Get petted by people around me
4. Watch movies
5. Play games
6. Read Rocket Around and other books
7. Chew on toys
8. Streeeeetch
9. Look out the window to see what we're flying over
10. Planning our next adventure

Your Top 10

1. _____
2. _____
3. _____
4. _____
5. _____
6. _____
7. _____
8. _____
9. _____
10. _____

German Phrases

German is the most widely spoken language in Switzerland. Out of the country's 26 cantons (sort of like states), 19 are German-speaking.

English	**German**
Hello	Hallo
How are you today?	Wie geht es dir heute
My name is	Wie heissen Sie
Can you help me	Kannst du mir helfen
Where is	Wo ist
I am lost	Ich bin verloren
I love to rocket around	Ich liebe es, durch die Gegend zu rasen
How do you say in English?	Wie sagst du das auf Englisch
Good bye!	Auf Wiedersehen!
What is your name?	Ich heiße (ß is called an eszett and sounds like 'sha')

French Phrases

The French language is spoken in the "Suisse Romande" – which is the western part of Switzerland. And includes the cantons of Geneva, Jura, Neuchâtel, and Vaud.

English	French
Hello	Bonjour
How are you today?	Comment allez-vous aujourd'hui
My name is	Mon nom est
What is your name?	Quel est ton nom
Can you help me	Pouvez-vous m'aider
Where is	Où est
I am lost	Je suis perdu
I love to rocket around	J'aime faire des fusées
How do you say in English?	Comment dites-vous en anglais
Good bye!	Au revoir!

Italian Phrases

In the canton of Ticino and in four valleys in the Canton of Graubünden, Italian is the main language spoken. A language called Rhaeto, and French, are also spoken in Graubünden.

English	**Italian**
Hello	Ciao
How are you today?	Come stai oggi
My name is	Mi chiamo
What is your name?	Come ti chiami
Can you help me	Mi potete aiutare
Where is	Dov'è
I am lost	Mi sono perso
I love to rocket around	Adoro sfrecciare in giro
How do you say in English?	Come si dice in inglese
Good bye!	Arrivederci!

Scavenger Hunt Switzerland

Find each of the below things in the pictures in this book or on your adventure in Switzerland (answers on next page)

In Lausanne

Market staircase (Escaliers du Marche)
Church of Saint Francois in Lausanne
Gold stones in front of Church of Saint Francois

In Lucerne

Chapel Bridge (Kappelbrücke)
Mill Square (Mühlenplatz)
Spreuer Bridge (Spreuerbrücke)
Swiss Museum of Transport
Mount Bürgenstock
A funicular
Mount Pilatus
An air gondola

In Zurich

Limmat river
Colorful houses
Clock

ANSWERS to Scavenger Hunt Switzerland

Find each picture of the below things in this book or find each
of the below things in Switzerland

In Lausanne

Market staircase (Escaliers du Marche) - Page 13
Fondue, Page 14
Gold stones in front of Church of Saint Francois - Page 16

In Lucerne

Chapel Bridge (Kappelbrücke) - Page 20
Mill Square (Mühlenplatz) - Page 19
Spreuer Bridge (Spreuerbrücke) - Page 19
Swiss Museum of Transport - Page 22
Mount Bürgenstock - Page 23
A funicular - Page 22
Mount Pilatus - Page 25
An air gondola - Page 24

In Zurich

Limmat river - Page 28
Colorful houses - Page 29
Big clock - Page 28

What Else to Do and See When You Rocket around Switzerland

Check each one you would like to see!

Geneva:

____ Animal petting zoo at Le Bois de la Bâtie

____ Giant chess pieces in Bastions Park

____ Playgrounds at the Parc de La Perle du Lac

____ The Reformation Wall

Lausanne:

____ Detective Badger

____ Space of Inventions

Lucerne:

____ Glacier Garden Lucerne (Gletschergarten)

____ Mt. Rigi

____ Natur-Museum Luzern

____ The Dying Lion of Lucerne – Löwendenkmal)

Zurich:

____ FIFA World Football Museum

____ Kunsthaus Zurich – Museum of Modern Art

____ Swiss National Museum

____ Take the tram around the city

____ Zurich Tram Museum

Other cities

Appenzell ____

Arosa ____

Basel ____

Bellinzona ____

Bern ____

Chur ____

Grindelwald ____

Guarda ____

Interlaken ____

Lugano ____

Montreux ____

Saint Moritz ____

Sion ____

St. Galen ____

Thun ____

Winterthur ____

Zermatt ____

Be a Rocketarounder!

--Read Rocket Around Switzerland AND do the activities --Join Rocket in building your brain through adventure, imagination, and finding new ways to have fun!

--Let Rocket's human family know: Where should Rocket and his humans go next? Where would your dog want to rocket-around with Rocket? (make sure your mom or dad are okay with it first). Email your ideas to lee@rocketaround.com

If you did these things, GREAT JOB!
You are an official Rocketarounder...
welcome to the Club!

I'M A ROCKETAROUNDER!

I build my brain through:

-Adventure
-Imagination
-Finding new ways to have fun!

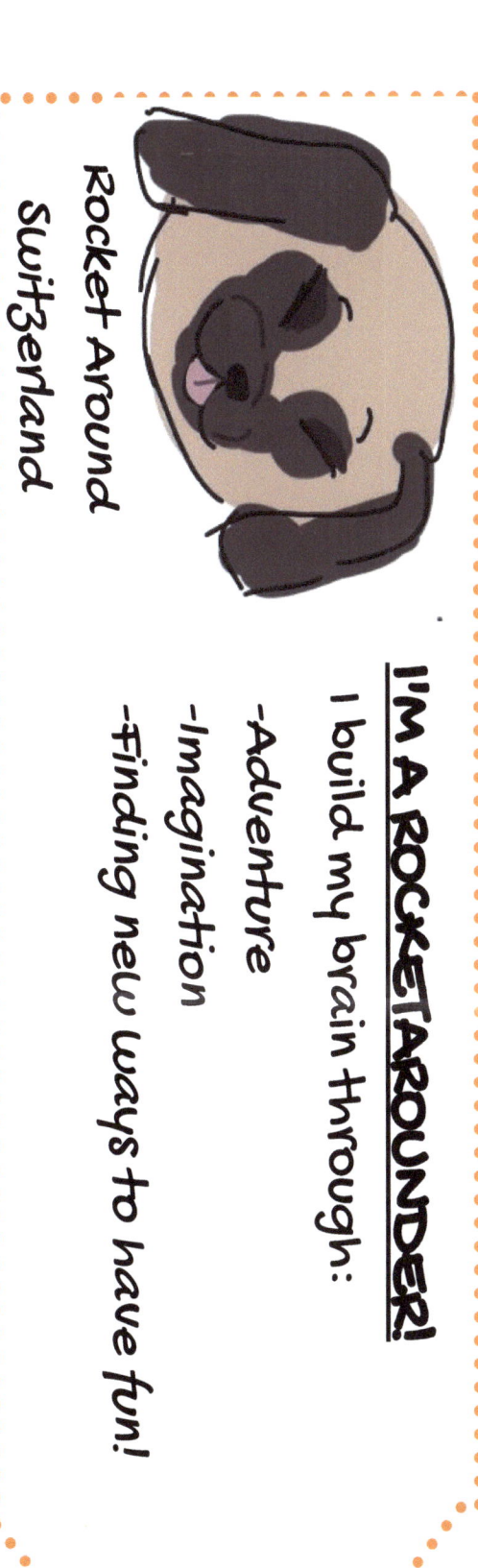

Rocket Around
Switzerland

The Humans + Rocket

Rocket is real, and
he lives with his
awesome
neurodiverse family
(his words, not ours)
in Alexandria, VA.

They love adventure
and traveling,
reading, writing,
sports, music, chess,
anime, chewing
sticks and toys, and
sleeping.

They hope you
enjoyed this book
and that you'll read
the next one!

More from Rocket Around

Books:

Rocket Around Washington DC – a neurodiverse visual guide with activities

Rocket Around Washington DC – a neurodiverse storybook

Rocket Around Washington DC! Neurodiverse activity + coloring book

Rocket Around Washington DC Ebook

Rocket Around Switzerland - A neurodiverse-friendly visual guide with activities

Rocket Around Switzerland - Neurodiverse-friendly storybook

Rocket Around Switzerland! Neurodiverse-friendly activity + coloring book

On the Internet:

Rocketaround.com blogsite on adventure & life for neuodiverse families

Facebook - https://www.facebook.com/groups/rocketaround

Instagram - https://instagram.com/rocketaroundtheglobe?igshid=YmMyMTA2M2Y=)

Pinterest - https://www.pinterest.com/rocketaround/

ISBN: 979-8-9889331-4-4

Printed in the U.S.A.

Look for other Rocket Around books and kids' activities at rocketaround.com!